Stitch Collection
Filet Crochet

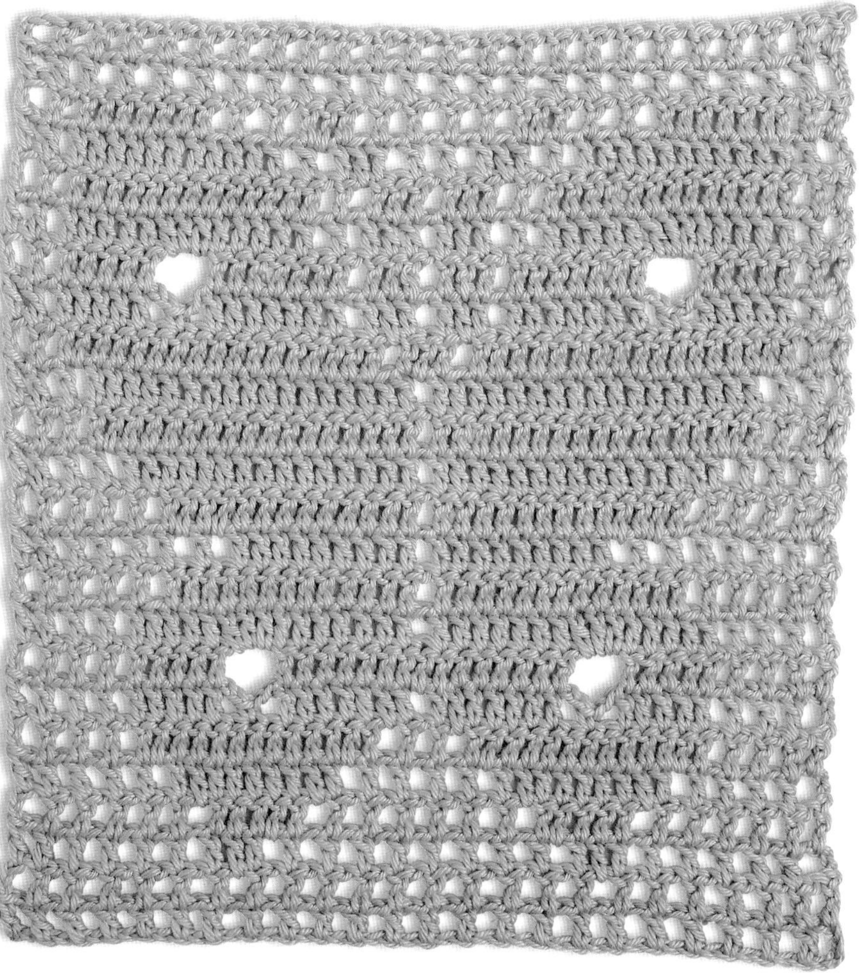

Stitch Collection

Filet Crochet

More than 70 designs
with easy-to-follow charts

Betty Barnden

St. Martin's Griffin
New York

Filet Crochet Stitch Collection.
Copyright © 2007 Quarto Inc.

For information, address St. Martin's
Press, 175 Fifth Avenue, New York,
N.Y. 10010.

www.stmartins.com

Library of Congress
Cataloging-in-Publication Data
Available Upon Request

ISBN-10: 0-312-37374-0
ISBN-13: 978-0-312-37374-0

QUAR: FCSC

First published in the United States by
St. Martin's Griffin

Conceived, designed and produced by
Quarto Publishing plc
The Old Brewery
6 Blundell Street
London N7 9BH

Project Editor: Lindsay Kaubi
Art Editor: Natasha Montgomery
Designer: Andrew Easton
Assistant Art Directors: Penny Cobb,
Caroline Guest
Illustrators: John Woodcock,
Coral Mula
Photographers: Philip Wilkins
Proofreader: Nicky Gyopari
Indexer: Helen Snaith

Art Director: Moira Clinch
Publisher: Paul Carslake

Manufactured in Singapore by
PICA Digital

Printed in China by 1010 Printing
International Ltd

First U.S. Edition: September 2007

10 9 8 7 6 5 4 3 2 1

Contents

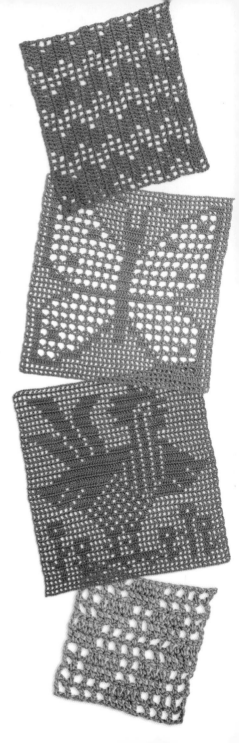

Introduction

Filet crochet was first developed as a method of making lace-like trimmings for dresses and household linens, using very fine threads (cotton or linen) and small steel crochet hooks.

"Filet" is the French word for "net," but in English the term is applied to crochet worked as a regular, square mesh with certain squares filled by blocks of extra stitches to form a design or pattern. The designs are normally presented in the form of simple charts, and once the basic methods of forming "blocks" and "spaces" are understood, these charts are very easy to follow.

About this book

Filet crochet know-how (pages 8–31)

This section of the book covers all the knowledge needed to begin filet crochet and work the designs in the book, beginning with choosing hooks and yarns and how to work the basic stitches. The basic meshes for filet crochet (small, medium, and large mesh) are explained in detail, along with how to read the filet charts.

Special techniques

Special filet techniques are also described in the Know-how section, such as working stepped edges, lacets, bars, and diamond lacets: these techniques are more unusual, so study these pages before beginning any design where they are required. To enable you to create your own filet crochet project, information on shaping, planning your own designs, and blocking and assembling crochet are included.

Design selector (pages 32–35)

These pages show all the samples in the Design collection in the form of a visual index, so you can quickly compare designs and choose the ones that you want.

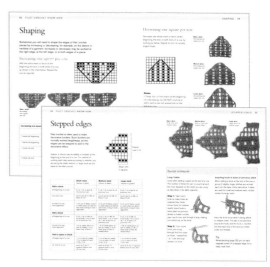

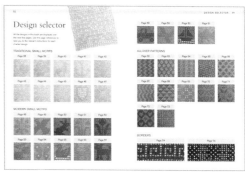

Fold-out flap

Opposite page 95 you'll find a handy fold-out flap featuring an instant reference on working filet crochet charts. You can leave it open while you work through the book.

Design collection (pages 38–92)

This directory includes 24 small motifs, 12 allover patterns, 11 border designs and four large designs as well as filet designs for the alphabet and numbers to use as you wish. Each design is presented in the form of a chart, with a photograph of a worked sample, and suggestions for combining the designs in different ways.

A crocheted sample shows the finished design

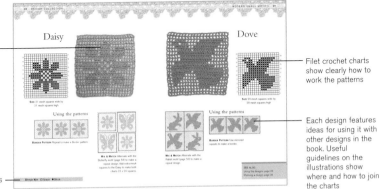

Filet crochet charts show clearly how to work the patterns

Each design features ideas for using it with other designs in the book. Useful guidelines on the illustrations show where and how to join the charts

A stitch key shows at-a-glance which stitches are needed for the design

A word about colors

CONTEMPORARY COLORS
Cream and white are traditional color choices for filet crochet but dark colors can be just as effective.

White, cream, and pastel shades are the traditional choice for filet crochet, with the work displayed against a dark background to show off the design to its best advantage.

However, you can also use brighter colors where they will be seen against a contrasting background, for example, a lined purse or pillow cover. Dark colors may be displayed against light, for example in a window treatment. It is always a good idea to experiment with a small sample before beginning a large project, to make sure the color and size of mesh will suit the design.

Filet crochet is fun to work, and surprisingly speedy. With the wide range of crochet and knitting yarns available today, there's plenty of scope for experimentation, so try out a few small designs in different yarns and colors to find out what appeals to you. Above all, have fun!

Hooks, yarns, and gauge

Filet crochet is traditionally worked with fine yarn and a small hook. However, there's no reason why you can't work with heavier yarns and large hooks, to suit your project.

Hooks

Hooks may be made of steel (small sizes), aluminum, wood, or plastic. Some have plastic handles or a flattened shaft for a better grip. Choose the hook recommended on the ball band of the yarn you want to use, or refer to the table opposite.

Yarns

As a general rule, yarns for filet crochet should be smooth and tightly spun. Fine crochet threads are usually cotton (or linen). For a larger mesh, try knitting yarns, available in wool, cotton, and other fibers. Avoid fluffy, knobbly, and fancy yarns, as these tend to obscure the detail of a filet design.

A selection of plastic and aluminum hooks.

Gauge

Gauge depends on the hook and yarn you use, how tightly you work, and on which mesh you choose: small, medium, or large (see page 16).

Cotton and linen, yarns are ideal for filet crochet.

• Work a small test piece (say, 10 x 10, or 20 x 20 mesh squares) with your chosen yarn and hook using small, medium, or large mesh, and block as described on page 30.
• Count the number of mesh squares in each direction to 4" (10cm). Then you can figure out how large a particular design panel will be, or calculate how many mesh squares you need to match a particular measurement.
• To make the mesh smaller (more squares to 4" (10cm)): try again with a smaller hook.
• To make the mesh larger (less squares to 4" (10cm)): try again with a larger hook.

Count the number of mesh squares in each direction to 4" (10cm).

Accessories

Only a few other tools are required for filet crochet:
- Tape measure for measuring gauge, and measuring work in progress
- Tapestry needles (with a large eye and blunt tip) for sewing seams and running in yarn tails
- Small scissors
- Rustproof pins

Hooks, yarns, and gauge guide

Always check your own gauge with the exact hook and yarn you intend to use for your project.

Yarn description	Typical gauge: number of mesh squares to 4" (10cm) (rough guide only)			U.S. steel hook sizes	U.S. plastic or aluminum hook sizes	International metric hook sizes
	Small mesh	Medium mesh	Large mesh			
crochet thread no. 100, tatting thread	30–40	20–27	18–24			.6mm
crochet thread nos. 70, 80	26–30	18–24	16–22	14		.75mm
				13		
crochet thread nos. 30, 40, 50, 60	24–32	17–23	15–20	12		1mm
				11		
crochet thread nos. 20, 30	21–25	16–21	14–18	10		1.25mm
				9		
crochet thread no.10, bedspread weight	19–25	14–20	12–16	8		1.5mm
				7		
crochet thread no. 5, heavy-weight bedspread, 2-ply, light fingering	16–20	12–15	10–13	6		1.75mm
				5		
				4		
3-ply, fingering	13–16	10–13	9–12	3		2mm
				2	B	2.25mm
				1		2.5mm
				0		
4-ply, fingering, sport	11 -14	8–11	7–9	00	C	2.75mm
					D	3mm
sport, DK, light worsted	9–11	6–8	5–7		E	3.5mm
					F	
					G	4mm
worsted, afghan, aran	6–8	5–7	4–6			4.5mm
					H	5mm
					I	5.5mm
chunky, bulky	5–7	4–6	3–5		J	6mm
					K	6.5mm
						7mm
super chunky, super bulky	3–5	2–4	1–3		L	8mm
					M	9mm
					N	10mm

Getting started

There are different ways to hold the hook and yarn; choose what's most comfortable for you.

Holding the hook

Hold the hook in your right hand if you are right-handed. You can hold it like a pencil (A), or with the shaft controlled by your fingers, like a table knife (B).

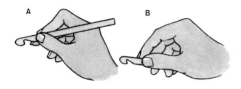

Making a slipknot

Step 1: Loop the yarn as shown, about 4–6" (10–15cm) from the end. Use the hook to catch the yarn leading to the ball and pull it through the loop.

> ### Tip
> If you are left-handed, look at these illustrations reflected in a mirror. Hold the hook in your left hand and the yarn in your right.

Step 2: Pull gently on both ends to tighten the knot against the hook.

Holding the yarn

Step 1: If you are right-handed, hold the yarn in your left hand. Wind the yarn around your fingers as shown to keep it slightly tensioned.

Step 2: As you work the stitches, use the hook to catch the yarn in front of your left forefinger and pull it through the loop already on the hook. The yarn should slip between your fingers without becoming loose.

Basic stitches

Filet crochet uses only a few basic crochet stitches. Described here are those stitches you need to learn to make the designs shown in this book.

Chain stitch *(abbr. ch)*

All filet crochet begins with a foundation chain of a certain number of stitches, and at the beginning of every row a certain number of turning chains are required. In filet work, chain stitches are also used to form the horizontal bar at the top of a filet space.

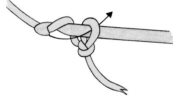

Step 1: Hold the hook and yarn as shown on page 10. Use the hook to catch the yarn so that it is wrapped around the throat of the hook in the direction shown. Pull a new loop through the loop of the slipknot: one chain made.

Step 2: Tighten the slipknot by pulling gently on the short yarn tail. Repeat until you have made the number of chains you need. Don't count the loop on the hook (or the slipknot).

Slip stitch *(abbr. ss)*

A slip stitch is the smallest crochet stitch you can make. In filet crochet, it is only used when working stepped edges (page 24).

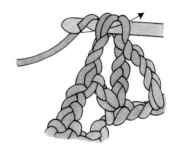

Step 1: Insert the hook under two threads at the top of the required stitch. Catch the yarn with the hook.

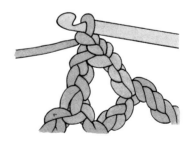

Step 2: Pull a new loop through the three loops on the hook. One slip stitch made.

Single crochet *(abbr. sc)*

This stitch is used in filet crochet when working lacets (page 22) and also for seams and edgings (pages 30–31).

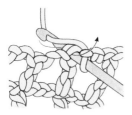

Step 1: Insert the hook where required (it is shown here inserted into the top of a double crochet, beneath two threads at the top of the stitch), making three loops on the hook. Catch the yarn with the hook and pull a new loop through, beneath the two threads of the stitch below.

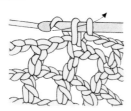

Step 2: Catch the yarn again, and pull a new loop through both loops on the hook.

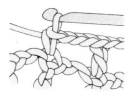

Step 3: One loop remains on the hook. One single crochet made.

Double crochet *(abbr. dc)*

Double crochet is used when working both small mesh and medium mesh (page 16).

Step 1: Wrap the yarn once around the hook as shown, then insert the hook where required. When working into the foundation chain, as shown here, insert the hook beneath two threads of a chain. On subsequent rows, when working into a previous double crochet, insert the hook beneath the two threads at the top of the stitch. Sometimes the hook is inserted into a chain space (see page 15).

Step 2: Catch the yarn with the hook and pull it through beneath the two threads (or through the chain space), making a third loop on the hook. Then catch the yarn again and pull it through the first two loops on the hook.

Step 3: Catch the yarn again and pull it through the two remaining loops on the hook. One loop remains on hook. One double crochet made.

Treble *(abbr. tr)*

This stitch is used when working large mesh (page 16).

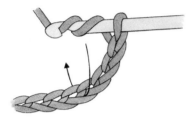

Step 1: Wrap the yarn twice around the hook, and insert the hook where required. On the first row, this will be in the foundation chain, as shown here, beneath two threads of the chain. On subsequent rows, the hook may be inserted into the top of a previous treble (beneath two threads at the top of the stitch), or into a chain space (see page 15).

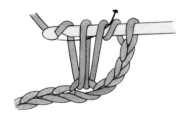

Step 2: Catch the yarn and pull a new loop through, beneath the two threads (or through the chain space), making a fourth loop on the hook. Then catch the yarn again and pull it through the first two loops on the hook.

Step 3: Catch the yarn again, and pull a new loop through the next two loops.

Step 4: Catch the yarn again and pull it through the two remaining loops on the hook. One loop remains on hook. One treble crochet made.

Basic techniques

The basic mesh for filet crochet may be small mesh, medium mesh, or large mesh, as described on page 16. Whichever mesh you choose, there are a few basic techniques common to all three.

Beginning a row

Every row begins with a number of chains, called the turning chain. For small and medium mesh, work three turning chains as shown here. For large mesh, work four turning chains (see page 16).

Note that in filet crochet, if the first chart square is a space, one or two more chains will be added after the turning chain, to form the bar at the top of the space.

Tip

If the edges of your work look uneven, try working one less turning chain than given for your chosen mesh.

Ending a row

Step 1: At the end of a row, the final double or treble crochet is always worked into the last turning chain. If you are working above a space on the previous row, be sure to skip the chains made for the top of the space and insert the hook into the last turning chain. Insert the hook under two threads of the chain and work the required stitch.

Step 2: Now turn the work around in your hands to work back along the next row. Always turn the work counter-clockwise to avoid twisting the turning chain at the beginning of the next row.

Working into a chain space

Step 1: When you are working a block above a space, you need to work one stitch for small mesh, or two stitches for medium mesh and large mesh (see page 16) into the space below the chains. Don't work into the chains themselves; the stitches will lie more neatly if you insert the hook through the chain space.

Step 2: Here, two double crochet have been worked into the chain space below.

Fastening off

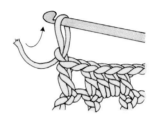

To fasten off at the end of the work, complete the final double or treble crochet of the mesh, then work one chain. Cut the yarn (never break it; always use scissors), leaving a tail of at least 4" (10cm), and pull the tail through the loop on the hook to secure.

BOAT MOTIF (PAGE 60)
This motif is worked in small mesh (see page 16) with lacets and bars (see page 22) to represent waves.

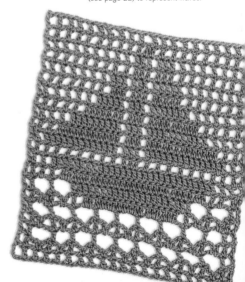

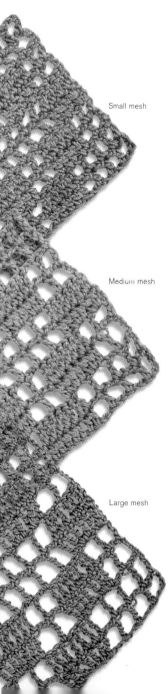

Small mesh

Medium mesh

Large mesh

Mesh patterns

Filet crochet charts may be interpreted using any of these three basic mesh patterns. Try out a small sample in each mesh to see which you prefer.

Small mesh

This is the easiest mesh pattern to follow, it works best in a crisp smooth yarn such as mercerized cotton. In softer, fuzzier yarns the stitch definition may be lost and the motif or pattern will become less visible.

Note Where several blocks are worked one after another, there will always be a run of odd-numbered double crochets. For example, 3 blocks = 6 dc, plus the final dc of the previous space, making a run of 7 dc.

Medium mesh

This is the classic mesh pattern, often used for traditional filet lace patterns. Depending on the yarn, hook, and your own personal gauge, you may find it difficult to produce a square mesh: it is often slightly "squashed." Correct blocking, as shown on page 30 can help to correct this problem.

Note Where several blocks are worked one after another, there will always be a multiple of 3 dc, plus 1. For example, 3 blocks = 9 dc, plus the final dc of the previous space, making a run of 10 dc.

Large mesh

This mesh is the most reliably square, and gives the best contrast between open spaces and solid blocks, making it suitable for any yarn. However, the resulting mesh fabric can be rather open and so it may be more suitable for decorative rather than practical projects.

Note Where several blocks are worked one after another, there will always be a run of a multiple of 3 tr, plus 1. For example, 3 blocks = 9 tr, plus the final tr of the previous space, making a run of 10 tr.

How to read charts

Each square on a chart represents either a "space" or a "block." These are worked in different ways for the small, medium, or large mesh patterns, shown opposite, and described in the table below.

Depending on the mesh you choose, a space is formed by working one or two chains followed by a double or treble crochet. A block is formed by working two or three double or treble crochets. Begin each row with the turning chain. Then work each space or block as given. Work the final stitch of the second and every following row into the last turning chain of the previous row, and turn the work.

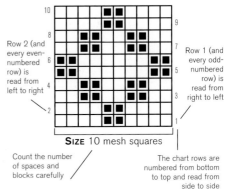

Row 2 (and every even-numbered row) is read from left to right

Row 1 (and every odd-numbered row) is read from right to left

SIZE 10 mesh squares

Count the number of spaces and blocks carefully

The chart rows are numbered from bottom to top and read from side to side

STITCH KEY □ Space ■ Block

	Small mesh (shown in pink)	Medium mesh (shown in blue)	Large mesh (shown in green)
Foundation chain: for each chart square on row 1 make	2 ch	3 ch	3 ch
First row: work turning chain	3 ch	3 ch	4 ch
if the first square is a space	1 ch, 1 dc in 6th ch from hook	2 ch, 1 dc in 8th ch from hook	2 ch, 1 tr in 9th ch from hook
each following space along row	1 ch, skip 1 ch, 1 dc in next ch	2 ch, skip 2 ch, 1 dc in next ch	2 ch, skip 2 ch, 1 tr in next ch
if the first square is a block	1 dc in 4th ch from hook, 1 dc in next ch	1 dc in 4th ch from hook, 1 dc in each of next 2 ch	1 tr in 5th ch from hook, 1 tr in each of next 2 ch
each following block along row	1 dc in each of next 2 ch	1 dc in each of next 3 ch	1 tr in each of next 3 ch
Following rows: work turning chain	3 ch, skip dc at base of this ch	3 ch, skip dc at base of this ch	4 ch, skip tr at base of this ch
for each space above a space	1 ch, skip 1 ch, 1 dc in next dc	2 ch, skip 2 ch, 1 dc in next dc	2 ch, skip 2 ch, 1 tr in next tr
for each space above a block	1 ch, skip 1 dc, 1 dc in next dc	2 ch, skip 2 dc, 1 dc in next dc	2 ch, skip 2 tr, 1 tr in next tr
for each block above a block	1 dc in each of next 2 dc	1 dc in each of next 3 dc	1 tr in each of next 3 tr
for each block above a space	1 dc in 1-ch space, 1 dc in next dc	2 dc in 2-ch space, 1 dc in next dc	2 tr in 2-ch space, 1 tr in next tr
at end of row work	last dc in 3rd of 3 turning ch, turn	last dc in 3rd of 3 turning ch, turn	last tr in 4th of 4 turning ch, turn

Shaping

Sometimes you will need to shape the edges of filet crochet pieces by increasing or decreasing; for example, on the sleeve or neckline of a garment. Increases or decreases may be worked at the right edge, at the left edge, or at both edges of a piece.

Increasing one square per row

Add one extra mesh or block at the beginning, the end, or both ends of a row, as shown in the chart below. Repeat the row as required.

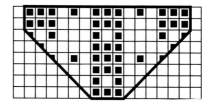

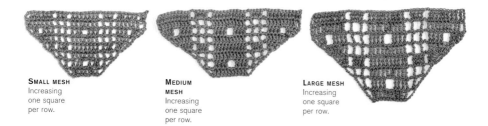

SMALL MESH Increasing one square per row.

MEDIUM MESH Increasing one square per row.

LARGE MESH Increasing one square per row.

Increasing one square per row			
	Small mesh (shown in pink)	**Medium mesh** (shown in blue)	**Large mesh** (shown in green)
1 mesh at beginning	5 ch, 1 dc in last st of previous row	6 ch, 1 dc in last st of previous row	7 ch, 1 tr in last st of previous row
1 block at beginning	4 ch, 2 dc in last st of previous row	4 ch, 3 dc in last st of previous row	5 ch, 3 tr in last st of previous row
1 mesh at end	[1 dc, 1 ch, 1 tr] in 3rd turning ch (4th turning ch when repeating the row)	[1 dc, 2 ch, 1 tr] in 3rd turning ch (4th turning ch when repeating the row)	[1 tr, 2 ch, 1 dtr] in 4th turning ch (5th turning ch when repeating the row)
1 block at end	[2 dc, 1 tr] in 3rd turning ch (4th turning ch when repeating the row)	[3 dc, 1 tr] in 3rd turning ch (4th turning ch when repeating the row)	[3 tr, 1 dtr] in 4th turning ch (5th turning ch when repeating the row)

Decreasing one square per row

Decrease one whole mesh or block at the beginning, the end, or both ends of a row, by working as below. Repeat to form an acutely angled slope.

Decreasing one square per row.

Decreasing one square per row.

Notes

• Three, four, or five chains at the beginning of a decreasing row DO NOT count as a stitch, and so are not worked into on the following row.
• Where two, three, or four stitches are worked together, the top of this stitch forms the first (or last) stitch of the row.

Decreasing one square per row.

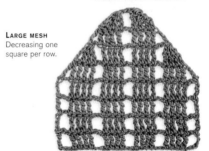

Decreasing one square per row			
	Small mesh (shown in pink)	**Medium mesh** (shown in blue)	**Large mesh** (shown in green)
1 mesh at beginning	3 ch, skip first 2 sts, 1 dc in next dc	4 ch, skip first 3 sts, 1 dc in next dc	5 ch, skip first 3 sts, 1 tr in next tr
1 block at beginning	3 ch, skip first st, 2 dc tog over next 2 sts	3 ch, skip first st, 3 dc tog over next 3 sts	4 ch, skip first st, 3 tr tog over next 3 sts
1 mesh at end	work 2 sts tog: [1 dc in 3rd last st, tog with 1 tr in last st]	work 2 sts tog: [1 dc in 4th last st, tog with 1 tr in last st]	work 2 sts tog: [1 tr in 4th last st, tog with 1 dtr in last st]
1 block at end	work 3 sts tog: [2 dc tog with 1 tr] over last 3 sts	work 4 sts tog: [3 dc tog with 1 tr] over last 4 sts	work 4 sts tog: [3 tr tog with 1 dtr] over last 4 sts

Special techniques

Working two or more stitches together

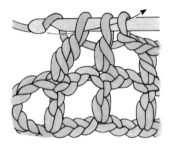

To work two stitches together, work the first stitch up to the final "yrh, pull through 2 loops," then the second stitch up to the final "yrh, pull through 2 loops." Yrh, pull through three loops on hook. Here, one double crochet is being worked together with one treble crochet.

To work three or more stitches together, work each stitch up to the final "yrh, pull through 2 loops" in the same way. Then work "yrh, pull through all loops on hook."

USING THE SHAPING TECHNIQUES

The neckline of this filet crochet jacket decreases by one square on every alternate row. The single crochet edging (page 31) evens out the steps.

For a more gradual slope

Sometimes you need to shape crochet more gradually; for example, when shaping a sleeve or an armhole.

Calculate how many squares need to be increased or decreased, and over how many rows, to give the gradual slope you want. For example, to decrease six squares over 12 rows you need to decrease one square at each end of every fourth row three times; or one square at one end only of every alternate row six times. Work one increase or decrease row as described, then work one or more rows without shaping. Repeat this sequence of rows as required.

The small mesh (pink) has been increased at each end of every third row. The medium mesh (blue) has been decreased at each end of every fourth row. The slightly stepped edges may be hidden in a seam (see pages 30–31) or straightened by adding a border (see page 27).

SMALL MESH
Increased at the end
of every third row.

MEDIUM MESH
Decreased at the end
of every third row.

Lacets, bars, and diamond lacets

These variations on the basic mesh are worked across two chart squares, making larger holes in the work to add variety to a design of blocks and spaces.

A lacet forms a v-shape, spanning two chart squares. Normally, a bar is worked directly above a lacet, on the next row. Lacets and bars may be worked in vertical or horizontal lines, side by side to fill a whole area, or singly to emphasize a detail such as a flower center. Lacets and bars were originally developed as a way of holding a ribbon or cord to gather filet crochet into a frill. A diamond lacet is formed by working the usual v-shaped lacet on one row, then on the next row a reverse lacet (an upside-down v-shape) directly above it, making a diamond-shaped hole.

Depending on the mesh chosen, a lacet is formed across two squares by working a number of chains, one single crochet into the double or treble crochet between the two squares, then the same number of chains again and a final double or treble crochet. On the next row, a bar is formed by working the number of chains required to span two chart squares, followed by a final double or treble crochet.

A reverse lacet is made up of one or two chains, then two double crochet together (or 2 tr tog, or 2 dtr tog) to complete the diamond shape, followed by one or two chains and a final double or treble crochet.

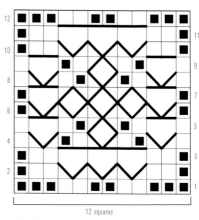

12 squares

Stitch key

⋎ Lacet   𝈁 Reverse lacet

▬ Bar

Tips
• When working the row above a bar, work into the chain space below the bar, not into the chains forming the bar.
• When working the row above a reverse lacet, work into the diamond-shaped space below the two stitches worked together, not into the two stitches worked together at the top of the reverse lacet.

SMALL MESH
Lacets and diamond lacets worked in small mesh.

MEDIUM MESH
Lacets and diamond lacets worked in medium mesh.

LARGE MESH
Lacets and diamond lacets worked in large mesh.

	Small mesh (shown in pink)	Medium mesh (shown in blue)	Large mesh (shown in green)
for each lacet above blocks or spaces (e.g. on chart row 2), or into foundation chain	2 ch, skip 1 st, 1 sc in next st, 2 ch, skip 1 st, 1 dc in next dc	3 ch, skip 2 sts, 1 sc in next st, 3 ch, skip 2 sts, 1 dc in next st	4 ch, skip 2 sts, 1 sc in next st, 4 ch, skip 2 sts, 1 tr in next st
for each bar above a lacet (e.g. on chart row 3)	3 ch, skip [2 ch, 1 sc, 2 ch], 1 dc in next dc	5 ch, skip [3 ch, 1 sc, 3 ch], 1 dc in next dc	5 ch, skip [4 ch, 1 sc, 4 ch], 1 tr in next tr
for each lacet above a bar	2 ch, 1 sc into 3-ch space, 2 ch, 1 dc in next dc	3 ch, 1 sc in 5-ch space, 3 ch, 1 dc in next dc	4 ch, 1 sc in 5-ch space, 4 ch, 1 tr in next tr
for blocks or spaces above a bar	work all but final dc into 3-ch space, end 1 dc in next dc	work all but final dc into 5-ch space, end 1 dc in next dc	work all but final tr into 5-ch space, end 1 tr in next tr
reverse lacet (used to complete a diamond lacet, e.g. at center of chart row 5)	1 ch, 2 dc tog (inserting hook in same place as previous dc, then in next dc), 1 ch, 1 dc in same place as last insertion	2 ch, 2 tr tog (inserting hook in same place as previous dc, then in next dc), 2 ch, 1 dc in same place as last insertion	2 ch, 2 dtr tog (inserting hook in same place as previous tr, then in next tr), 1 ch, 1 tr in same place as last insertion
on the row above a reverse lacet	work into the diamond-shaped space, not into the 2 dc tog	work into the diamond-shaped space, not into the 2 tr tog	work into the diamond-shaped space, not into the 2 dtr tog

Threading ribbon through lacets and bars

A line of lacets and bars may be threaded with a ribbon and left flat, or gathered up to make a frill. See Lacet zigzag border, page 76.

Stepped edges

Filet crochet is often used to make
decorative borders. Such borders are
normally worked lengthways, so the
edges can be stepped to add to the
decorative effect.

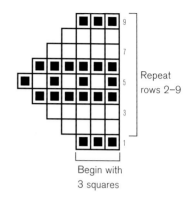

Repeat
rows 2–9

Spaces or blocks may be added, or omitted, at the
beginning or the end of a row. The method of
working each step varies according to whether you
are using the small, medium, or large mesh as the
basis for the filet crochet.

Begin with
3 squares

	Small mesh (shown in pink)	Medium mesh (shown in blue)	Large mesh (shown in green)
Add a space			
at beginning of a row	5 ch, 1 dc in last dc of previous row	7 ch, 1 dc in last dc of previous row	8 ch, 1 tr in last tr of previous row
(on next row)	(work last dc in 4th of these 5 ch)	(work last dc in 5th of these 7 ch)	(work last tr in 6th of these 8 ch)
at end of a row (see opposite)	1 ch, yrh 3 times, insert in same place as last dc and work a long tr (see opposite)	2 ch, yrh 4 times, insert in same place as last dc and work a long tr (see opposite)	2 ch, yrh 5 times, insert in same place as last tr and work a long tr (see opposite)
Add a block			
at beginning of a row	4 ch, 1 dc in 4th ch from hook, 1 dc in last dc of previous row	5 ch, 1 dc in 4th ch from hook, 1 dc in next dc, 1 dc in last dc of previous row	6 ch, 1 tr in 5th ch from hook, 1 tr in next ch, 1 tr in last tr of previous row
at end of a row (see opposite)	1 tr in same place as last dc made, 1 tr in base loop of this tr	1 tr in same place as last dc made, [1 tr in base loop of last tr made] twice	1 dtr in same place as last tr made, [1 dtr in base loop of last dtr made] twice
Omit a space or block			
at beginning of a row	1 ss in last dc made, 1 ss in each of next 2 sts, 3 ch	1 ss in last dc made, 1 ss in each of next 3 sts, 3 ch	1 ss in last tr made, 1 ss in each of next 3 sts, 4ch
at end of a row	work to 2 sts (1 square) before end of row, turn	work to 3 sts (1 square) before end of row, turn	work to 3 sts (1 square) before end of row, turn

SMALL MESH
Small mesh with
stepped edges.

MEDIUM MESH
Medium mesh with
stepped edges.

LARGE MESH
Large mesh with
stepped edges.

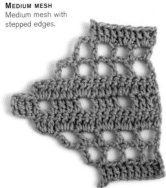

Special techniques

Used when adding a space at the end of a row.
The number of times the yarn is wound around
the hook depends on the mesh you are using,
as described in the table opposite.

Yarn round
hook as many times as
required (four times
shown here, for medium
mesh). Insert hook in
same place as previous
double or treble crochet,
yarn round hook, pull through a loop, making
one extra loop on the hook.

*Yarn round
hook, pull a loop
through first two loops
on hook, * repeat from
* to * until one loop
remains on hook

When adding a block at the end of the row, a
group of slightly longer stitches are worked,
each into the base of the one before. Trebles
are used for small and medium mesh, double
trebles for large mesh.

Here, the third extra treble is being added
to medium mesh. The yarn is wound twice
around the hook, and the hook is inserted
into the base loop of the previous treble,
under two threads.

Tip
When blocking (page 30), pin out each
separate corner of a stepped edge, for a
really neat finish.

Using the designs

Filet crochet may be used in many ways to make all sorts of projects, from a simple square purse to a delicate summer top or jacket.

PATCHWORK THROW
Join squares patchwork-style to make large items such as throws.

Small motifs and large designs

Most of the charts for small motifs (pages 38–61) and large designs (pages 82–89) are square, making them ideal for creating purses, pillow covers, and throws. Simply choose a suitable yarn and hook size to make any square the size you want (pages 8–9).

Two squares joined back-to-back will make a purse or pillow cover. Place the squares with wrong sides together and join with a single crochet seam (page 31) around the outside edges.

Square motifs may be joined patchwork-style to make large items such as pillow covers and throws. If the charts you choose are not exactly the same size, add extra mesh squares all around the smaller charts to match the size of the larger charts. Use either the flat-sewn seam (page 30) or the single crochet seam (page 31) to join the squares into strips, then join the strips together and add a double crochet or a filet crochet border (see opposite).

Allover patterns

Allover patterns (pages 62–73) contrast well with isolated motifs. Allover patterns are easy to use when shaping is required, because it is fairly simple to keep the pattern constant when shaping (see pages 18–20).

PURSE AND PILLOW COVER
Square motifs are ideal for creating purses and pillow covers. Simply join the squares back to back.

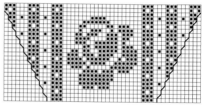

SHAPING ALLOVER PATTERNS
Combine motifs and allover patterns for shaped items.

Border patterns

Border patterns (pages 74–81) may be worked
separately and stitched to crochet, knitting, or
fabric. Borders with straight edges are easily
combined with other motifs and patterns.
Borders with stepped edges are worked
sideways. To edge crochet, knitting, or fabric
work a border to the length required without
fastening off. Stitch most of the border in place,
then adjust the length to match exactly before
fastening off and completing the stitching.

BORDERS
You can work borders separately and then join them to a
crochet, knit, or fabric article.

Working sideways

Sometimes it is convenient to work a design
sideways. Any chart of simple blocks and spaces
may be turned through 90 degrees, so that the
left or right edge becomes the
first row. Re-number the rows
along the new side edges.
Charts with stepped edges,
or lacets and bars, may not
be worked in this way.

WORKING SIDEWAYS
Two hearts motif rotated
through 90 degrees.

Working in negative

Change the look of any charted design by
working blocks instead of spaces, and vice versa.

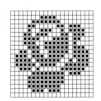 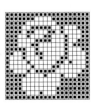

Stitching borders to fabric

To edge fabric, the
raw edge of the
fabric must first be
finished with a hem.

Machine-stitched hem

**Machine stitching or hand
stitching a hem**
Take the edge of
the fabric and fold
and press ¼" (6mm)
to the wrong side.
Then fold again by
at least ⅜" (9mm),
press again and pin

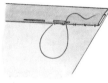

Hand-stitched hem

in place. Use matching thread to machine
stitch close to the first fold, through all
thicknesses of fabric. Or stitch by hand, taking
only tiny stitches through the single fabric
thickness, so that the stitches barely show on
the right side. Press the hem again.

**Stitching a
crochet border**
With right sides
facing, pin the hem
of the fabric so it
just overlaps the
straight edge of the
crochet border. Use

thread to match the fabric to stitch in place.

Straight crochet border as an insert
Borders with two straight
edges may be set
between two pieces
of fabric, using the
same method as for
stitching a border.

Planning a design

Combining charts

Suggestions for combining designs are given with each chart, but you can make up your own combinations too, to suit any project you have in mind.

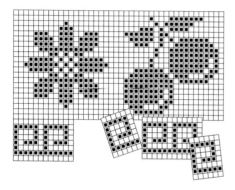

MAKING UP YOUR OWN CHART

Make up your own chart for a large project by photocopying several charts and taping them together onto a large sheet of paper, then work the crochet all in one piece. When joining the photocopies together, make sure all the grid squares match up exactly. Remember to number the rows.

Tip

- When photocopying charts, enlarge by any percentage you wish, to make it easier to number the rows.
- You can also copy charts with a computer and scanner.

Planning a complicated design

For a more complicated design the process is slightly different.

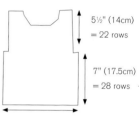

5½" (14cm) = 22 rows

7" (17.5cm) = 28 rows

10¼" (26cm) = 41 squares

First make a rough drawing of the piece you want and write the measurements on it. Then check your gauge and calculate how many mesh squares you need for each measurement (pages 8–9).

41 squares

Now draw the outline of the piece onto graph paper, with one square for each mesh square, and copy the designs into the position you want them. The gaps between motifs may be left as mesh squares, or you can add more patterns or small motifs in any arrangement you choose. Again, remember to number the rows.

Planning corners to work all in one piece

With careful planning, a border design (without stepped edges) may be added to two or more sides of another chart, and the whole worked as one piece.

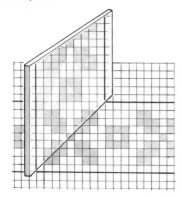

USE A MIRROR

To help you plan a corner, place a small mirror diagonally across any border chart. Then decide which part of the pattern forms the most pleasing corner, before drawing or joining together the whole chart.

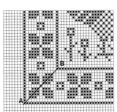

DRAWING UP THE CHART

The corner shown here is symmetrical either side of the diagonal line A–B. If necessary, add extra mesh squares to the center panel, so that the border fits the panel and each corner is the same.

Planning corners to work separately

Borders with stepped edges must be worked lengthways in separate sections and be stitched into place. Such borders also make a pretty edging for table linen. Borders without stepped edges may be worked this way too, making the edge of the work more stable than if the whole is worked in one piece.

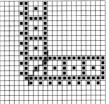

PLANNING STEPPED EDGE BORDERS

Plan the corner as shown right, drawing a stepped line at the corner to divide the border into sections.

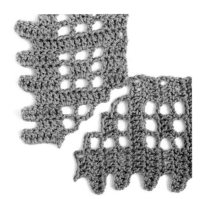

JOIN THE EDGES

Work each border section with steps (page 24) to match the dividing line. Join the border sections to the main panel, then join the corners with a flat-sewn seam (page 30).

Assembly

Careful finishing and assembly will show off your work to its best advantage.

Blocking

Before assembling filet crochet, the pieces should be blocked so that the mesh is square. This process evens out any slight inconsistencies of gauge, and sets the stitches in place.

You will need a bowl of water, a towel, a blocking board, a tape measure, and rustproof pins. For the blocking board use a well-padded ironing table, or cover a piece of board with a layer of batting and a layer of cotton fabric, tightly stretched and stapled in place. A blocking board about 24" x 30" (60 x 75cm) is useful for garment pieces, and covering it with gingham fabric helps to pin the pieces squarely.

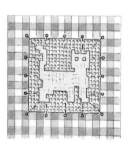

PINNING THE DESIGN
Pin around the edges of the crochet at regular intervals.

Immerse the crochet in a bowl of lukewarm water. Gently squeeze the water through it and leave it to soak for a couple of minutes to make sure it is thoroughly wet. Drain away the water and roll the crochet in a towel to blot away excess moisture.

Lay the crochet right side up on the blocking board and gently pat it flat to the correct measurements. Pin all around the edges at

intervals of no more than 2" (5cm), making sure the rows of mesh squares run straight. Leave to dry completely before removing the pins.

Flat-sewn seam

Edges to be joined should each have the same number of mesh squares. If the pieces are correctly blocked, the side edges of rows may be joined to a lower or upper edge and the squares will match exactly.

Use the same yarn as used for the crochet, and a tapestry needle to suit the yarn. This has a blunt tip, ensuring that the stitches pass between the threads without splitting them. You can start by threading up a tail left at the beginning or end of a piece, and join in new lengths as required.

SEWING SEAMS
Use a blunt-tipped needle for sewing seams.

With wrong sides upward, lay the two edges side-by-side on a flat surface. Pass the needle under one thread of the right edge, then under corresponding thread of the left edge, and pull through. Then pass the needle from left to right under the next pair of corresponding threads in the same way.

Repeat as required. The stitches form a zigzag from side to side. Make sure all the mesh squares match exactly.

Single crochet seam

A single crochet seam may be worked on either the right side of the work or the wrong side. It forms a small ridge, which can be decorative on the right side, especially if worked in a contrasting color.

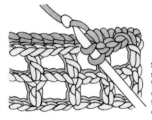

SINGLE CROCHET SEAM
Worked in a contrasting color, this seam can be decorative.

Hold the two edges with right sides or wrong sides together, as desired. Join the yarn to one corner with 1 ss, 1 ch. Work 1 sc through both corners together.
• For small mesh: work *1 sc through the next pair of chain spaces, 1 sc through next pair of row ends (or through next pair of dc)*, repeat from * to * to end.
• For medium and large mesh: work *2 sc through the next pair of chain spaces, 1 sc through next pair of row ends (or through next pair of dc or tr)*, repeat from * to * to end.

Single crochet edging

A simple single crochet edging may be worked all around a flat piece of filet crochet for a neat finish. Further rows or rounds of single crochet or other stitches may be added as desired.

EDGING
Work this edging all around a flat piece for a neat edge.

Work the same number of single crochet in the spaces and stitches as for a single crochet seam. At corners, work three single crochet in the same place. At the same time, you can work over any yarn tails so they are enclosed within the edging for about 2" (5cm), then pull gently on the yarn tail and snip off the excess with scissors.

Running in tails

Use a tapestry needle to run in any remaining yarn tails on the wrong side of the work, where they will not show.

Thread the tail into a tapestry needle and run it in and out, either along a seam, or through the backs of the crochet stitches for at least 2" (5cm). Snip off excess yarn.

Design selector

All the designs in this book are displayed over
the next few pages. Use the page references to
take you to the relevant instructions for each
charted design.

TRADITIONAL SMALL MOTIFS

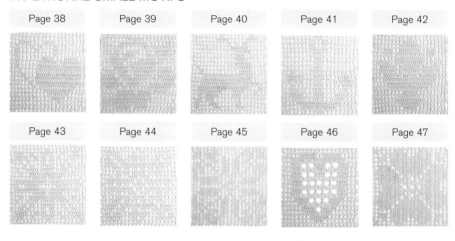

| Page 38 | Page 39 | Page 40 | Page 41 | Page 42 |

| Page 43 | Page 44 | Page 45 | Page 46 | Page 47 |

MODERN SMALL MOTIFS

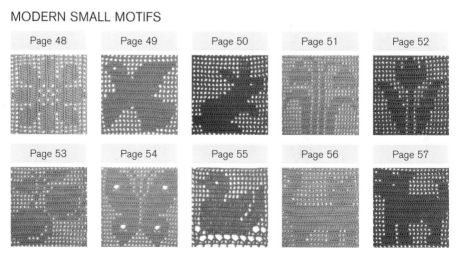

| Page 48 | Page 49 | Page 50 | Page 51 | Page 52 |

| Page 53 | Page 54 | Page 55 | Page 56 | Page 57 |

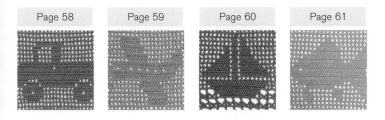

Page 58 Page 59 Page 60 Page 61

ALLOVER PATTERNS

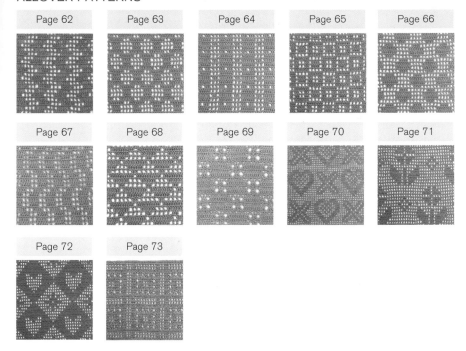

Page 62 Page 63 Page 64 Page 65 Page 66

Page 67 Page 68 Page 69 Page 70 Page 71

Page 72 Page 73

BORDERS

Page 74 Page 74

Page 75

Page 75

Page 76

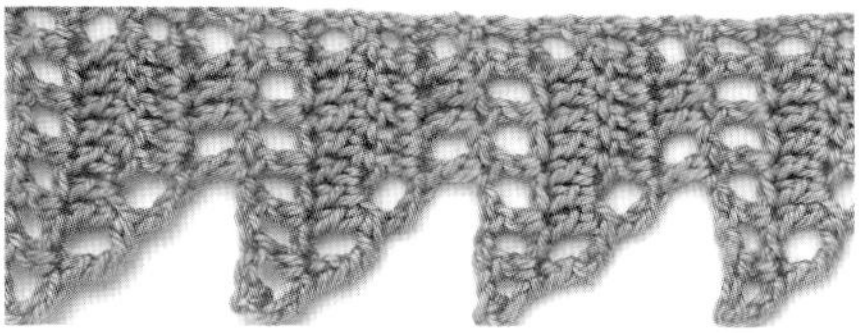

Page 76

Page 77

Page 78

Page 79

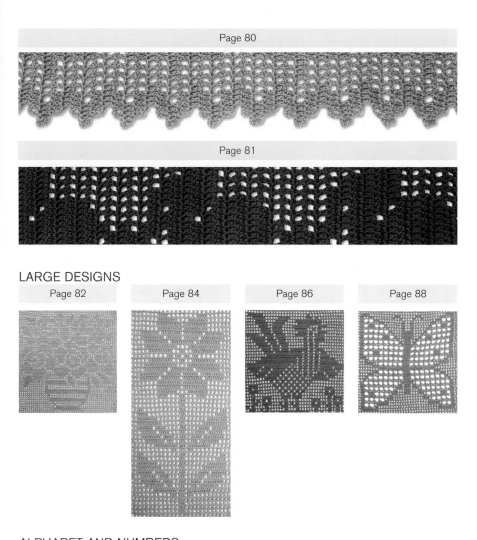

Page 80

Page 81

LARGE DESIGNS

Page 82

Page 84

Page 86

Page 88

ALPHABET AND NUMBERS

Page 90

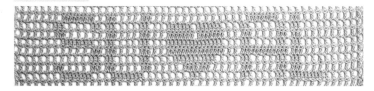

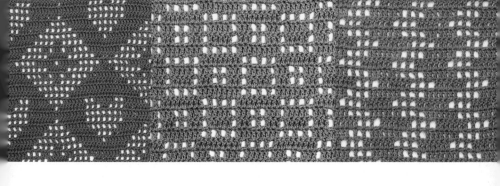

Design collection

The Design collection includes more than 70 filet crochet designs including small motifs, allover patterns, borders, large designs, the alphabet, and numbers. Each design is presented in the form of a chart, with a photograph of a worked sample, and suggestions for combining the designs in different ways.

Two hearts

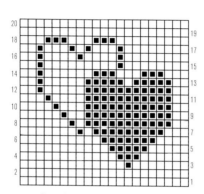

SIZE 21 mesh squares wide by
20 mesh squares high

Using the pattern

BORDER PATTERN Combine with the Dove motif
(page 49) to make a border pattern.

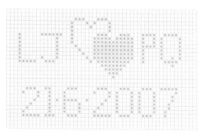

MIX & MATCH Add lettering
(page 90) to commemorate a
special occasion.

STITCH KEY   □ Space   ■ Block

Rose

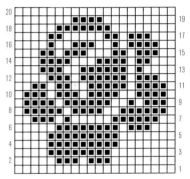

Size 20 mesh squares wide by
20 mesh squares high

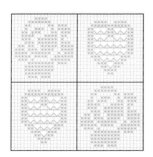

Mix & Match Alternate with
Lacet heart motif (page 46) for
a repeat design.

Using the pattern

Border Pattern Use mirrored repeats
to form a border.

SEE ALSO
Using the designs, page 26
Planning a design, page 28

Stag

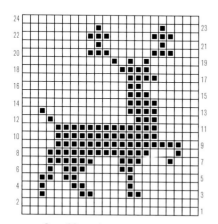

SIZE 22 mesh squares wide by
24 mesh squares high

Using the pattern

BORDER PATTERN Use mirrored
repeats to form a line of stags.

MIX & MATCH Combine with
the Star border (page 74).
Place 24 rows of Star border
between each pair of Stags.

STITCH KEY   □ Space   ■ Block

Anchor

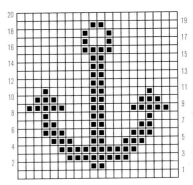

SIZE 20 mesh squares wide by
20 mesh squares high

Using the pattern

BORDER PATTERN Flip alternate
Anchor motifs upside down to make
a border pattern.

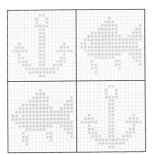

MIX & MATCH Alternate
with the Fish motif
(page 61) to form a
repeat design.

SEE ALSO
Using the designs, page 26
Planning a design, page 28

Fleur de Lys

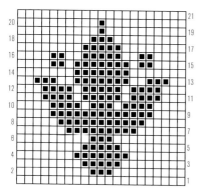

SIZE 21 mesh squares wide by
21 mesh squares high

Using the pattern

BORDER PATTERN Work the chart
sideways, adding the Small square
blocks border (page 75).

MIX & MATCH Alternate with
the Snowflake motif
(page 44) for a repeat design.

STITCH KEY ☐ Space ■ Block

Star

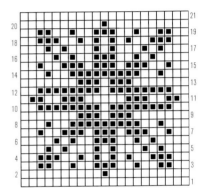

SIZE 21 mesh squares wide by
21 mesh squares high

Using the pattern

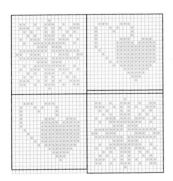

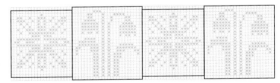

BORDER PATTERN Alternate with the Snowdrop
motif (page 51) to make a border pattern. Add extra
squares to the Star chart to match the height of
the Snowdrop chart.

MIX & MATCH Alternate with Two
hearts motif (page 38) for a repeat
design. Add extra mesh squares to
the Two hearts chart, to make both
charts 21 x 21 squares.

SEE ALSO
Using the designs, page 26
Planning a design, page 28

Snowflake

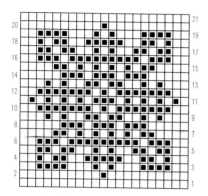

SIZE 21 mesh squares wide by
21 mesh squares high

Using the pattern

MIX & MATCH Make a repeat design
with the Star motif (page 43), and the
Daisy motif (page 48).

STITCH KEY ☐ Space ■ Block

Norwegian flower

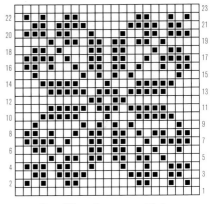

SIZE 23 mesh squares wide by
23 mesh squares high

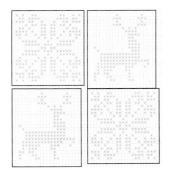

MIX & MATCH Alternate with the
Stag motif (page 40) for a repeat
design. Add extra mesh squares to
make both charts 24 x 24 squares.

Using the pattern

BORDER PATTERN Work the chart sideways,
adding the Lacet zigzag border (page 76).

SEE ALSO
Using the designs, page 26
Planning a design, page 28

Lacet heart

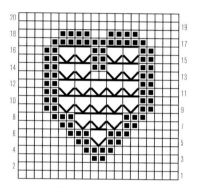

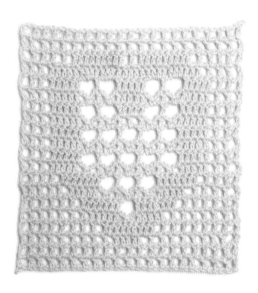

SIZE 20 mesh squares wide by
20 mesh squares high

Using the patterns

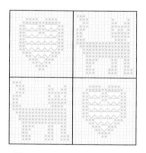

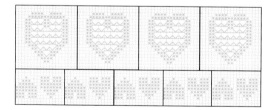

BORDER PATTERN Combine with the Small hearts
border (page 77). 4 repeats of Lacet heart = 5
repeats of Small hearts border, worked sideways.

MIX & MATCH Alternate with
the Cat motif (page 56) for a
repeat design.

STITCH KEY □ Space ■ Block ⊻ Lacet and bar ◪ Diamond lacet

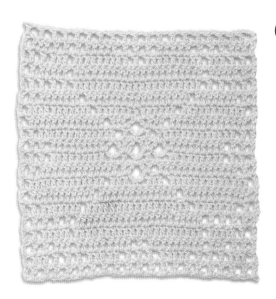

Geranium

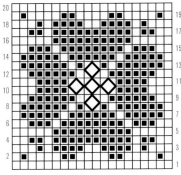

SIZE 20 mesh squares wide by
20 mesh squares high

Using the patterns

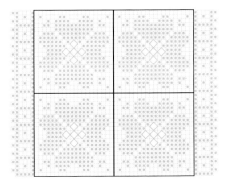

MIX & MATCH Make an allover
repeat design and add the Small
square blocks border (page 75).

SEE ALSO
Lacets, bars, and diamond
lacets, page 22
Using the designs, page 26
Planning a design, page 28

Daisy

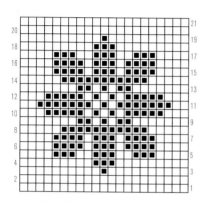

SIZE 21 mesh squares wide by
21 mesh squares high

Using the patterns

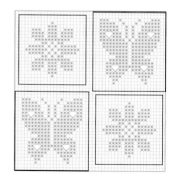

BORDER PATTERN Repeat to make a Border pattern.

MIX & MATCH Alternate with the Butterfly motif (page 54) to make a repeat design. Add extra mesh squares to the Daisy to make both charts 23 x 24 squares.

STITCH KEY □ Space ■ Block

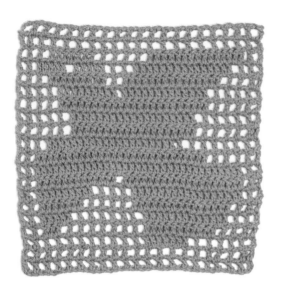

Dove

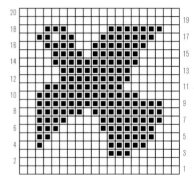

SIZE 20 mesh squares wide by
20 mesh squares high

Using the patterns

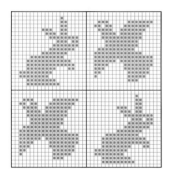

MIX & MATCH Alternate with the
Rabbit motif (page 50) to make a
repeat design.

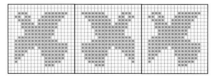

BORDER PATTERN Use mirrored
repeats to make a border.

SEE ALSO
Using the designs, page 26
Planning a design, page 28

Rabbit

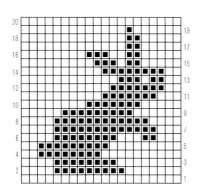

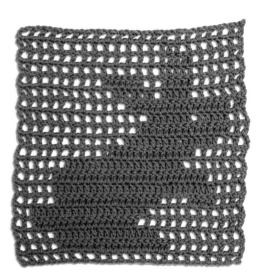

Size 20 mesh squares wide by
20 mesh squares high

Using the patterns

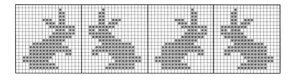

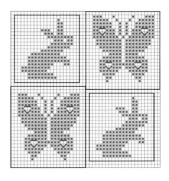

Border Pattern Use mirrored repeats to form a
line of rabbits.

Mix & Match Alternate with the
Butterfly motif (page 54). Add
extra mesh squares to the Rabbit.

Stitch Key ☐ Space ■ Block

Snowdrop

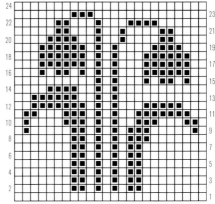

SIZE 24 mesh squares wide by
24 mesh squares high

Using the patterns

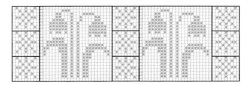

BORDER PATTERN Add bands of Stars from the
border on page 74. 3 Stars = 24 squares = height
of Snowdrop chart.

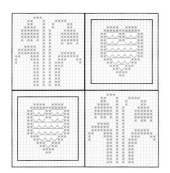

MIX & MATCH Alternate with Lacet
heart motif (page 46). Add extra
mesh squares to make both charts
24 x 24 squares.

SEE ALSO
Using the designs, page 26
Planning a design, page 28

Tulip

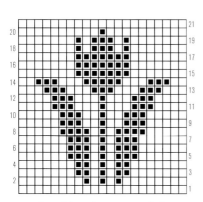

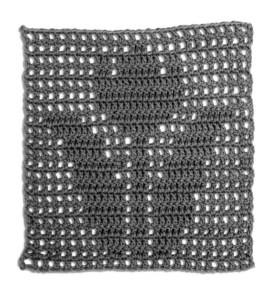

SIZE 21 mesh squares wide by
21 mesh squares high

Using the patterns

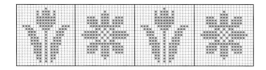

BORDER PATTERN Alternate with the Daisy motif
(page 48) for a border or allover repeat pattern.

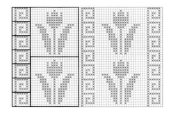

MIX & MATCH Work in
vertical bands with the Greek key
border (page 74). Height of 2
Tulips = 42 squares = 7 repeats
of Greek key border.

STITCH KEY □ Space ■ Block

Cherries

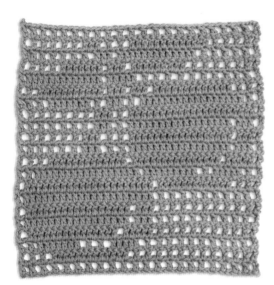

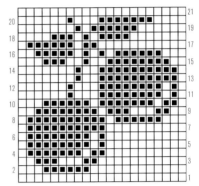

SIZE 21 mesh squares wide by
21 mesh squares high

Using the patterns

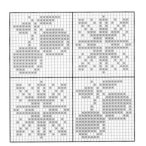

MIX & MATCH Alternate with
the Star motif (page 43) for a
repeat design.

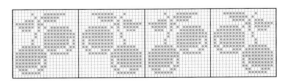

BORDER PATTERN Use mirrored repeats to make
a border pattern.

SEE ALSO
Using the designs, page 26
Planning a design, page 28

Butterfly

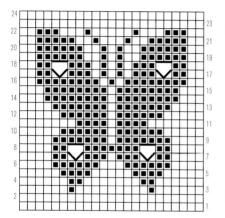

SIZE 23 mesh squares wide by
24 mesh squares high

Using the patterns

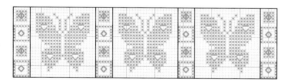

BORDER PATTERN Repeat with vertical bands
of Lacet square border (page 75). Height of
Butterfly chart = 24 squares = 2 repeats of
Lacet square border.

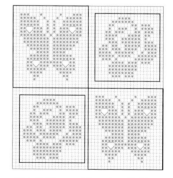

MIX & MATCH Alternate with Rose
motif (page 39). Add extra mesh
squares to the Rose motif to make
both charts 23 x 24 squares.

STITCH KEY □ Space ■ Block ☑ Lacet and bar

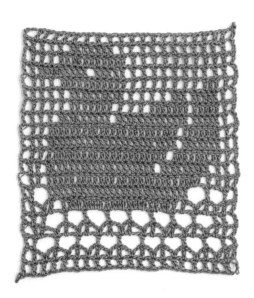

Duck

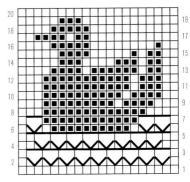

Size 20 mesh squares wide by
20 mesh squares high

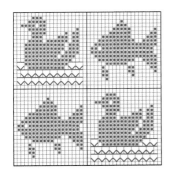

Mix & Match Alternate with
the Fish motif (page 61) for a
repeat design.

Using the patterns

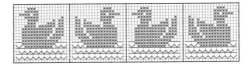

Border Pattern Use mirrored repeats to form a
line of ducks.

SEE ALSO
Lacets, bars, and diamond lacets,
page 22
Using the designs, page 26
Planning a design, page 28

Cat

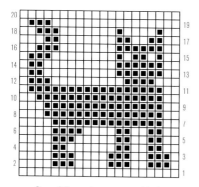

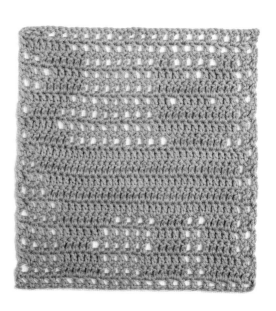

Size 20 mesh squares wide by
20 mesh squares high

Using the patterns

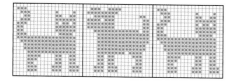

Border Pattern Alternate with the Dog motif
(opposite), for a border or repeat design.

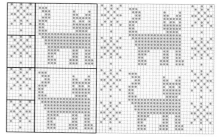

Mix & Match Work in vertical bands with
the Star border (page 74). The height of 2 Cat
charts = 40 squares = 4 repeats of Star border.

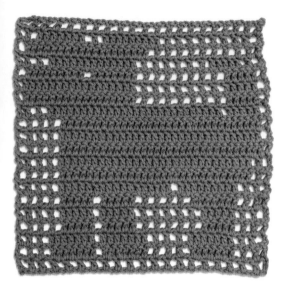

Dog

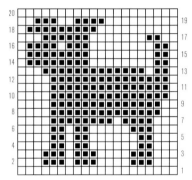

SIZE 20 mesh squares wide by
20 mesh squares high

Using the patterns

MIX & MATCH Make a repeat design
with the Cat (opposite) and the Rabbit
(page 50).

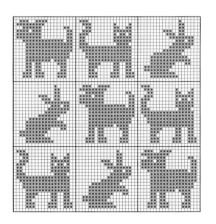

SEE ALSO
Using the designs, page 26
Planning a design, page 28

Pickup truck

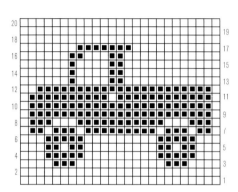

SIZE 25 mesh squares wide by 20 mesh squares high

Using the patterns

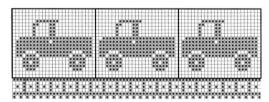

BORDER PATTERN Working sideways, repeat the Pickup truck motif, adding the Small square blocks border (page 75).

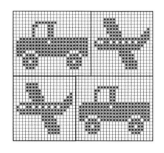

MIX & MATCH Alternate with the Plane motif (opposite) for a repeat pattern.

STITCH KEY ☐ Space ■ Block

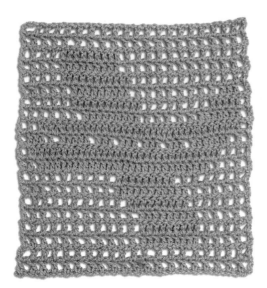

Plane

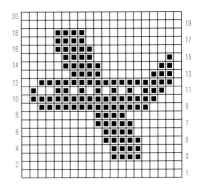

SIZE 20 mesh squares wide by
20 mesh squares high

Using the patterns

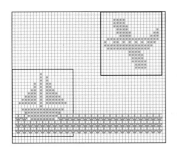

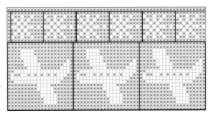

MIX & MATCH Make a seascape
with the Boat motif (page 60),
continuing the lacet pattern across
the whole width to represent water.

BORDER PATTERN In
negative, repeat the Plane
motif, adding the Star
border (page 74) worked
sideways. The width of 3
Plane charts = 60 squares
= 6 repeats of Star border.

SEE ALSO
Using the designs, page 26
Working sideways, page 27
Working in negative, page 27
Planning a design, page 28

Boat

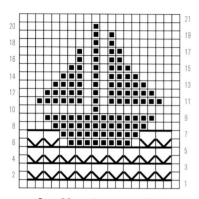

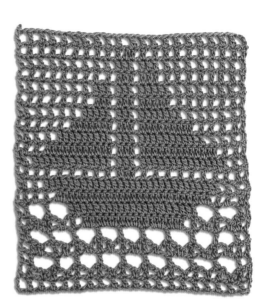

SIZE 20 mesh squares wide by
21 mesh squares high

Using the patterns

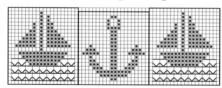

BORDER PATTERN Alternate with the Anchor
motif (page 41). Add extra mesh squares
to the Anchor chart to make both charts
20 x 21 squares.

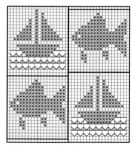

MIX & MATCH Alternate with the
Fish motif (opposite) for a repeat
design. Add extra squares to the
Fish chart to to make both charts
20 x 21 squares.

STITCH KEY □ Space ■ Block ⊻ Lacet and bar

Fish

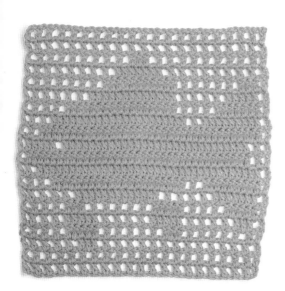

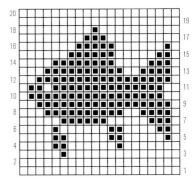

SIZE 20 mesh squares wide by
20 mesh squares high

Using the patterns

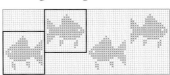

BORDER PATTERN Use mirrored repeats to form a
whole school of fish. Add extra squares to the Fish
chart, so that the fish appear at different heights.

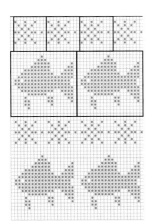

MIX & MATCH Work in stripes with the Star border
(page 74). Width of 2 Fish charts = 40 squares =
4 repeats of Star border, worked sideways.

SEE ALSO
Lacets, bars, and diamond lacets,
page 22
Using the designs, page 24
Working sideways, page 27
Planning a design, page 28

Zigzags

REPEAT these
6 mesh squares

Start with a multiple of 6 mesh squares.
Repeat the 4 rows as required.

The pattern may also be worked
sideways, beginning with a multiple of
4 mesh squares.

Using the patterns

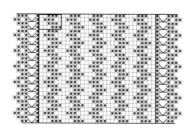

ADD A BORDER Add Lacet zigzag
border (page 76).

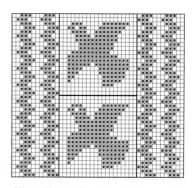

MIX & MATCH Combine with Dove motif
(page 49) in vertical bands.

STITCH KEY □ Space ■ Block

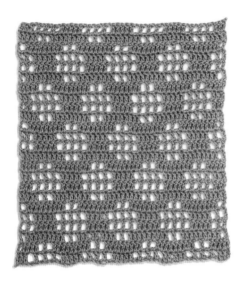

Trellis

REPEAT these
6 mesh squares

Start with a multiple of 6 mesh squares.
Repeat the 8 rows as required.

The pattern may also be worked
sideways, beginning with a multiple
of 8 mesh squares.

Using the patterns

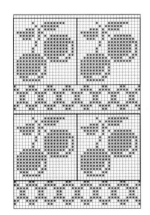

MIX & MATCH Just 8 rows of Trellis
makes a line of crosses, combined here
with Cherries motif (page 53).

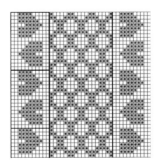

BORDER PATTERN
Work the pattern
in vertical bands,
divided by bands of
Small hearts border
(page 77).

SEE ALSO
Using the designs, page 26
Working sideways, page 27
Planning a design, page 28

Spotted stripe

Work once

REPEAT these
6 mesh squares

Begin with a multiple of 6 mesh
squares, plus 3. Repeat the 4 rows
as required.

This pattern may also be worked
sideways. Begin with a multiple of 4
mesh squares.

VARIATION Repeat to make a chart of
21 x 21 squares, then arrange 4
copies of this chart to make a
basketweave pattern.

Using the patterns

STITCH KEY   □ Space   ■ Block

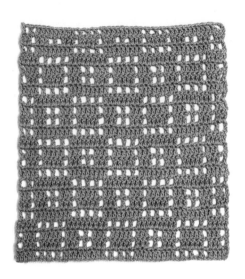

Checks

REPEAT these
8 mesh squares

Begin with a multiple of 8 mesh
squares and repeat the 8 rows
as required.

Using the patterns

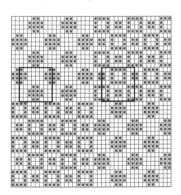

MIX & MATCH Repeat to make a chart
of 20 x 20 squares. Do the same with
Spots allover pattern (page 66), then
alternate the 2 squares.

SEE ALSO
Using the designs, page 26
Working sideways, page 27
Planning a design, page 28

Spots

REPEAT these
8 mesh squares

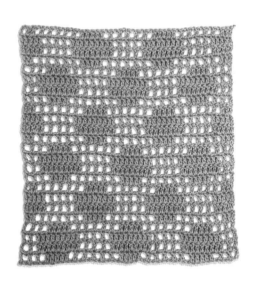

Start with a multiple of 8 mesh
squares. Repeat the 8 rows
as required.

Using the patterns

MIX & MATCH Combine vertical bands of
Spots allover pattern, 12 squares wide, with
bands of Two hearts motif (page 38).

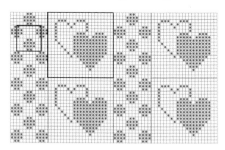

STITCH KEY   □ Space   ■ Block

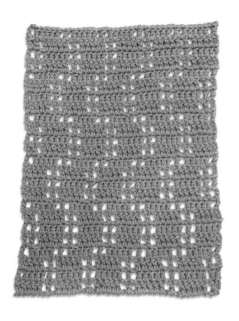

Waves

REPEAT these
4 mesh squares

Begin with a multiple of 4
mesh squares. Repeat the 8
rows as required.

Using the patterns

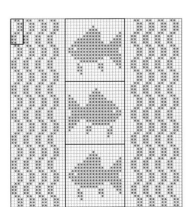

MIX & MATCH Work the pattern
in vertical bands, either side of Fish
motifs (page 61).

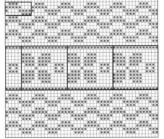

MIX & MATCH
Combine horizontal
bands (worked
sideways) with
bands of Flower
border (page 79),
also worked
sideways.

SEE ALSO
Using the designs, page 26
Working sideways, page 27
Planning a design, page 28

Triangles

Work once

REPEAT these
6 mesh squares

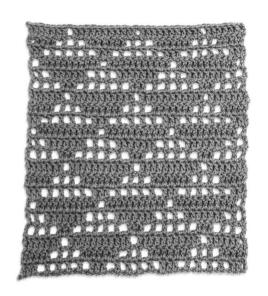

Begin with a multiple of 6 mesh
squares, plus 1. Repeat the 6 rows
as required, ending on row 3 or 6.

Using the patterns

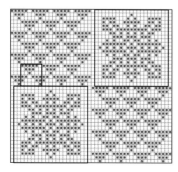

MIX & MATCH Repeat to make a chart of
24 x 24 squares and alternate with
Snowflake motif (page 44).

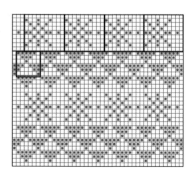

MIX & MATCH Work in horizontal
bands with Star border (page 74),
worked sideways.

STITCH KEY □ Space ■ Block ◪ Diamond lacet

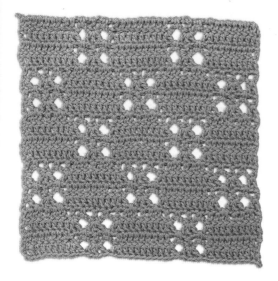

Lacet squares

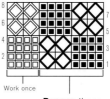

Work once

REPEAT these 6 mesh squares

Start with a multiple of 8 mesh squares, plus 4. Repeat the 8 rows as required, ending row 4 or 8.

Using the patterns

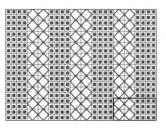

VARIATION Repeat chart rows 1–4 only to make vertical bands of pattern.

MIX & MATCH Repeat to make a chart of 20 x 20 squares, then alternate with the Geranium motif (page 47).

SEE ALSO
Lacets, bars, and diamond lacets, page 22
Using the designs, page 26
Working sideways, page 27
Planning a design, page 28

Hearts and kisses

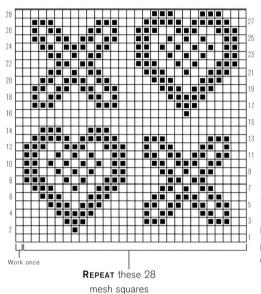

Work once

REPEAT these 28
mesh squares

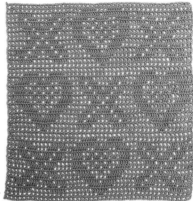

Begin with a multiple of 28 mesh squares, plus 1. Repeat the 28 rows as required, ending on row 15 or row 1.

Using the patterns

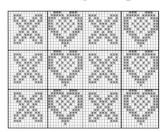

VARIATION Repeat rows 1–14 only to make a pattern with a vertical emphasis.

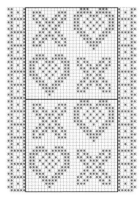

ADD A BORDER Add borders of Small square blocks (page 75). 7 repeats of Small square blocks = 1 lengthways repeat of Hearts and kisses.

STITCH KEY   □ Space   ■ Block

Cornflowers

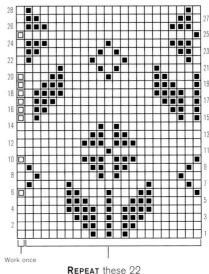

Start with a multiple of 22 mesh squares, plus 1. Repeat the 28 rows as required, ending on row 14 or 28.

Work once

REPEAT these 22 mesh squares

Using the patterns

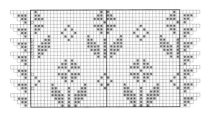

ADD A BORDER Add Small zigzag border (page 76). 7 repeats of Small zigzag border = 1 lengthways repeat of Cornflowers.

VARIATION Work the design in negative for a more solid fabric.

SEE ALSO
Using the designs, page 26
Working in negative, page 27
Planning a design, page 28

Hearts and daisies

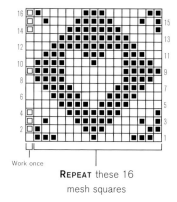

Work once

REPEAT these 16 mesh squares

Begin with a multiple of 16 mesh squares, plus 1. Repeat the 16 rows as required.

Using the patterns

MIX & MATCH Add bands of Small hearts border (page 77), worked sideways and in negative.

STITCH KEY   □ Space   ■ Block   ⊠ Diamond lacet

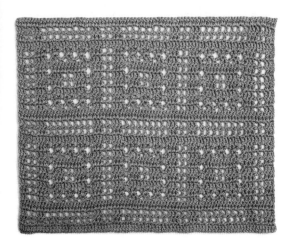

Lacet checks

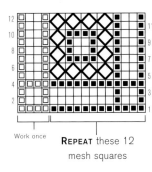

Start with a multiple of 12 mesh squares, plus 4. Repeat the 12 rows as required, preferably ending on row 4.

Work once   **REPEAT** these 12 mesh squares

Using the patterns

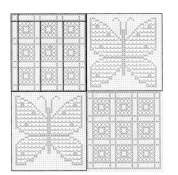

MIX & MATCH Repeat to form a chart of 40 x 40 squares, then alternate with the Large Butterfly design (page 88).

ADD A BORDER Repeat to form a chart of 40 x 40 squares. Add 1 square all around (making 42 x 42 squares), to fit Greek key border (page 74), arranged as shown.

SEE ALSO
Lacets, bars, and diamond lacets, page 22
Working sideways. page 27
Working in negative, page 27
Planning a design, page 28

Greek key

Using the patterns

SIZE Begin with 8 squares and repeat rows 1–6

This chart may be worked lengthways in the direction shown, or turned on its side and repeated sideways across the width of the work.

BORDER PATTERN Work two Greek key borders back to back, reversing the left-hand border.

Star

SIZE Begin with 9 squares and repeat rows 1–10

This chart may be worked lengthways in the direction shown, or turned on its side and repeated sideways across the width of the work.

Using the patterns

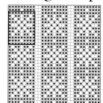

MIX & MATCH Work in negative, reversing the mesh squares and solid blocks (page 27) and alternate with open mesh stripes for an allover pattern.

STITCH KEY ☐ Space ■ Block ☒ Diamond lacet

Lacet square

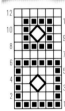

This chart may be worked lengthways in the direction shown, or turned on its side and repeated sideways across the width of the work.

SIZE Begin with 6 squares and repeat rows 1–12

Using the patterns

MIX & MATCH Work sideways (page 27) in stripes with the Stag from page 40. 2 repeats of Lacet square border = 1 Stag.

Small square blocks

SIZE begin with 5 squares and repeat rows 1–4.

This design may not be worked sideways because of the stepped edge. Repeat the 4 chart rows as required.

Using the patterns

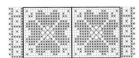

BORDER PATTERN Add side borders to the Geranium motif (page 47). 5 repeats of Small square blocks = 1 Geranium. Work the stepped edge as shown on page 24.

Small zigzag

This design may not be worked sideways because of the stepped edge. Work separately, then stitch to the lower edge of any design.

Using the patterns

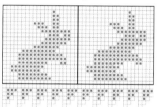

SIZE Begin with 3 squares and repeat rows 1–4

BORDER PATTERN Rabbit motif (page 50) shown here. 5 repeats of Small zigzag border = 1 Rabbit.

Lacet zigzag

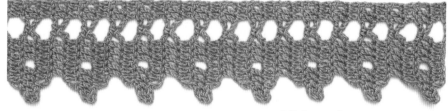

This design may not be worked sideways because of the stepped edge. Work separately, then stitch to the lower edge of any design.

Using the patterns

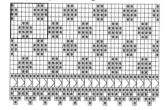

SIZE Begin with 5 squares and repeat rows 1–4

BORDER PATTERN Spots allover pattern (page 66) shown here, 2 repeats of Lacet zigzag border = 1 repeat of Spots pattern.

STITCH KEY ☐ Space ■ Block ☒ Lacet and bar

Small hearts

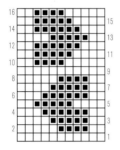

SIZE Begin with 11 squares and repeat rows 1–16

This chart may be worked lengthways in the direction shown, or turned on its side and repeated sideways across the width of the work.

Using the patterns

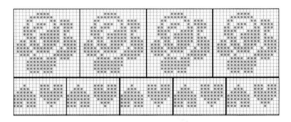

BORDER PATTERN Work sideways and combine with the Rose motif (page 39). 2½ repeats of Small hearts border = 5 Small hearts = 2 Roses.

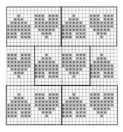

VARIATION Work sideways and repeat for an allover pattern.

SEE ALSO
Lacets, bars, and diamond lacets, page 22
Stepped edges, page 24
Working sideways, page 27

Snake

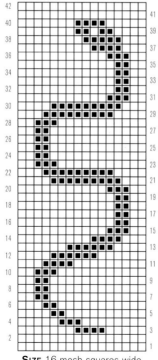

SIZE 16 mesh squares wide
by 42 mesh squares high

STITCH KEY ☐ Space ■ Block

Using the patterns

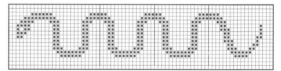

BORDER PATTERN You can repeat chart rows 15–30 as many times as you wish to make a snake of any length. This chart may also be turned on its side and worked sideways across the width of the work.

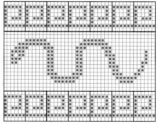

MIX & MATCH Work sideways in stripes with the Greek key border (page 74). 1 snake as charted = 7 repeats of Greek key border.

Flower

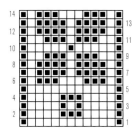

Using the patterns

SIZE Begin with 13 squares and repeat rows 1–14

This chart may be worked lengthways in the direction shown, or turned on its side and repeated sideways across the width of the work.

MIX & MATCH Work in vertical stripes with the Trellis pattern (page 63). 32 rows of Flower border = 4 repeats of Trellis pattern.

VARIATION Work the chart sideways in stripes, working in negative on alternate stripes.

SEE ALSO
Working in negative, page 27
Working sideways, page 27

Trees

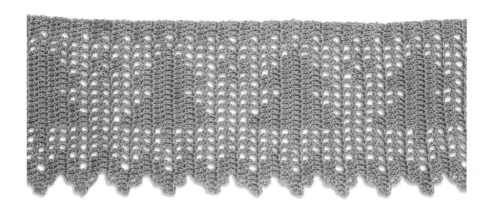

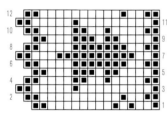

SIZE Begin with 16 squares and repeat rows 1–12

Repeat the 12 chart rows to length required. For the shaped edge to be symmetrical, end with chart row 1. This design may not be worked sideways unless you omit the stepped edge.

Using the patterns

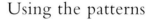

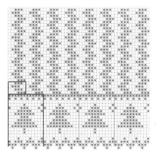

BORDER PATTERN Adjust the length to suit the width of any small allover pattern, such as the Zigzags (page 62) shown here. I Tree repeat = 2 repeats of Zigzag.

MIX & MATCH Omit the borders, and arrange single Trees, worked sideways, alternately with the Stag motif (page 40). Add extra mesh squares above and below the Trees.

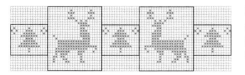

STITCH KEY □ Space ■ Block

Elephants

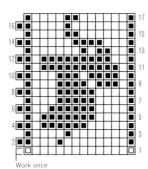

Work once

SIZE Begin with 11 squares and repeat rows 2–16

Work chart row 1, then repeat chart rows 2–17 as required, and end with chart row 1. This design may not be worked sideways unless you omit the stepped edge.

Using the patterns

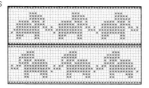

VARIATION Work sideways, omitting the stepped edge and repeating the Elephant across the width. Lines of elephants may face opposite directions.

BORDER PATTERN Adjust the length by adding 1 or more rows as chart row 1 at each end, to match the width of any small allover pattern, such as the Spotted stripe (page 64) shown here.

SEE ALSO
Stepped edges, page 24
Working sideways, page 27

Roses

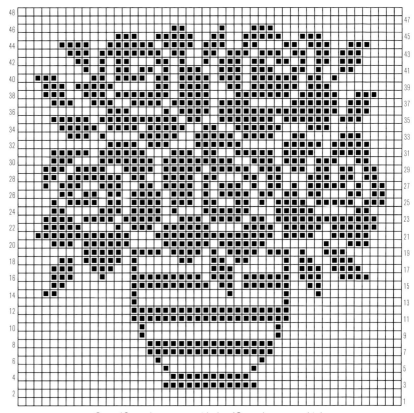

SIZE 48 mesh squares wide by 48 mesh squares high

Using the patterns

ADD A BORDER Add the Lacet square border (page 75) all around to make a panel 60 x 60 mesh squares.

MIX & MATCH Position 4 Lacet heart motifs (page 46) on a 48 x 48 grid of mesh squares, and alternate with the Roses design.

STITCH KEY □ Space ■ Block

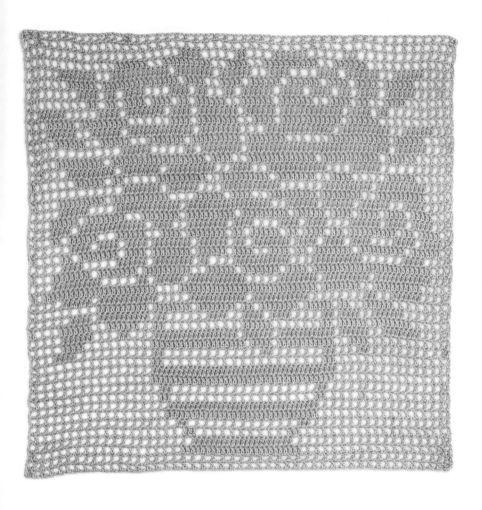

SEE ALSO
Lacets, bars, and diamond
lacets, page 22
Using the designs, page 24
Planning a design, page 28

Large flower

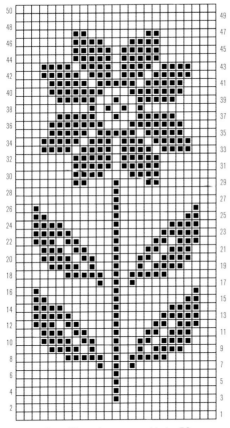

SIZE 25 mesh squares wide by 50 mesh squares high

Using the patterns

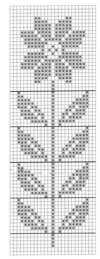

VARIATION Repeat rows 7–16 as many times as you like, to make a long, narrow panel.

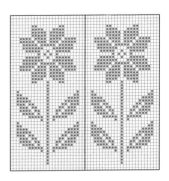

VARIATION Two Large flowers side by side make a panel of 50 x 50 mesh squares.

STITCH KEY □ Space ■ Block

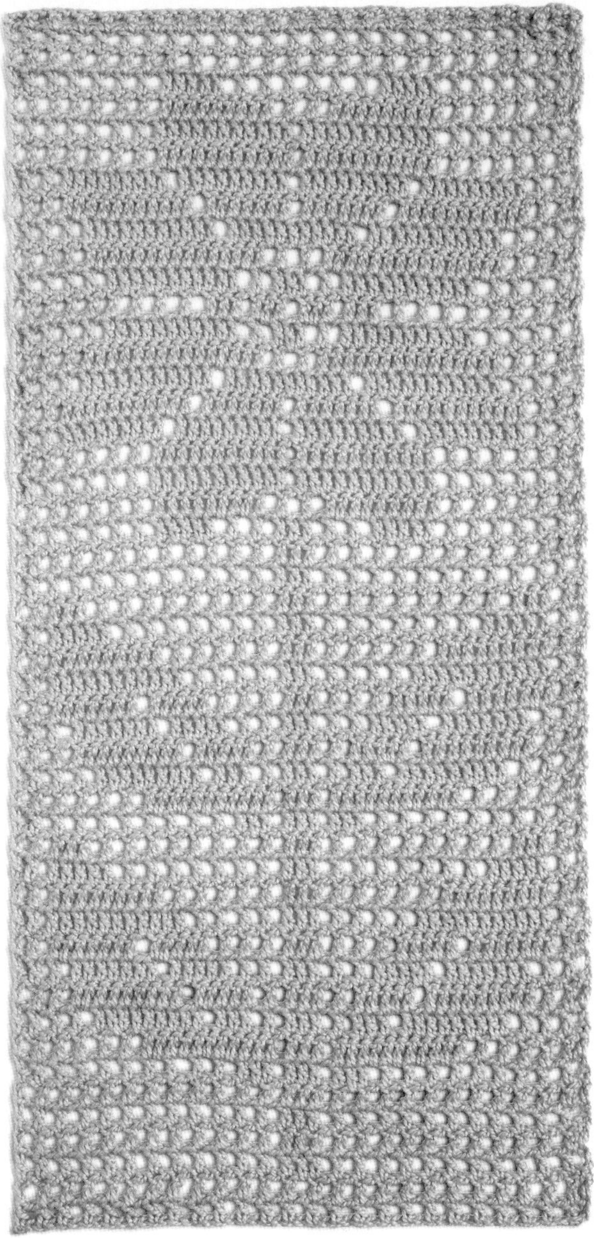

Rooster

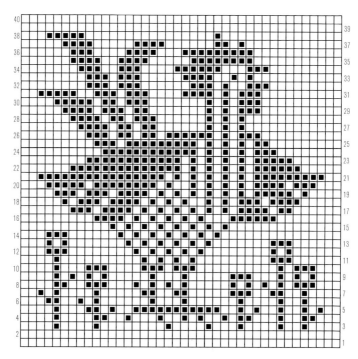

SIZE 40 mesh squares wide by 40 mesh squares high

Using the patterns

BORDER PATTERN
Repeat the design to make a row of Roosters, adding stripes of Star border (page 74), worked sideways. 4 repeats of Star border = 1 Rooster.

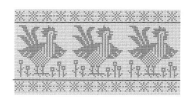

MIX & MATCH Alternate with blocks of Spots allover pattern (page 66).

STITCH KEY □ Space ■ Block

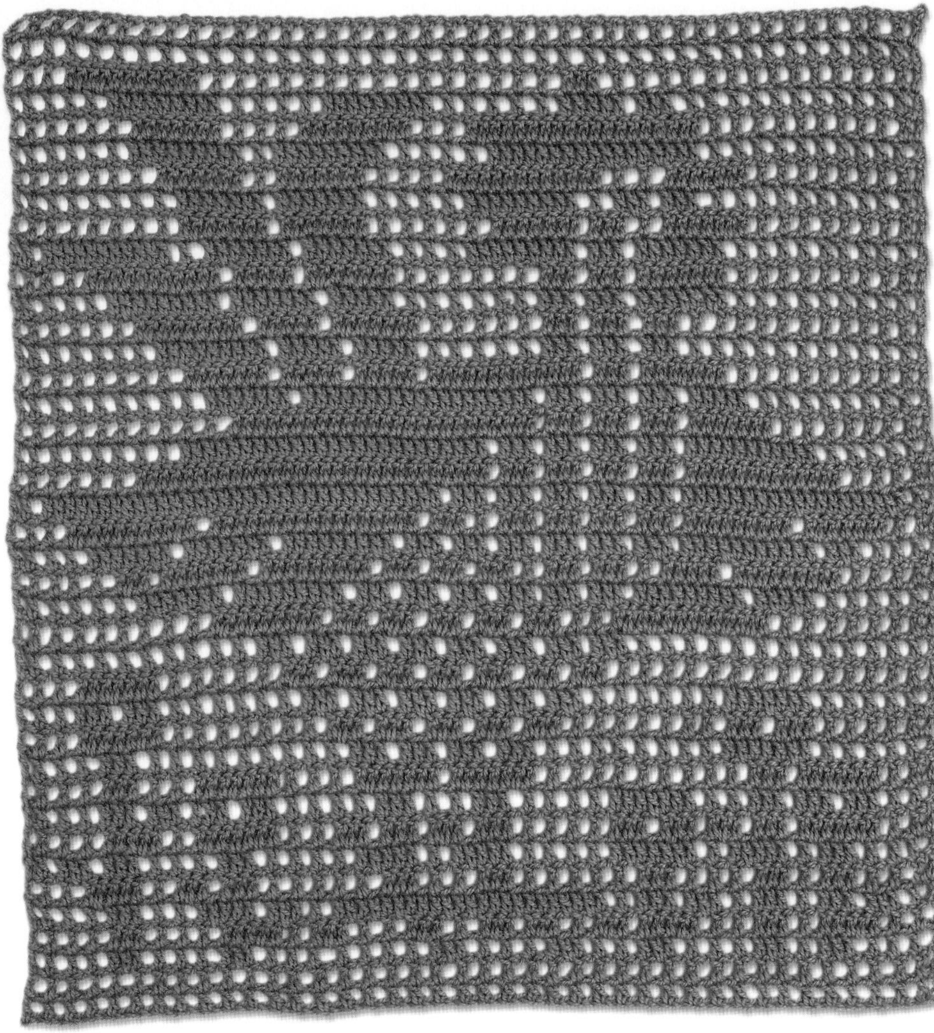

SEE ALSO
Using the designs, page 26
Planning a design, page 28

Butterfly

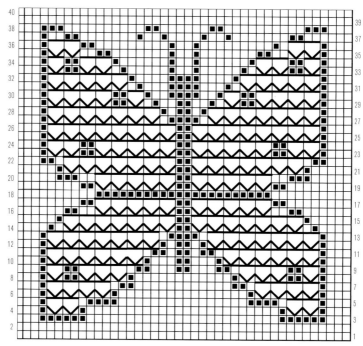

SIZE 40 mesh squares wide by 40 mesh squares high

Using the patterns

ADD A BORDER Add Small hearts border (page 77) all around the edges. 2½ repeats of Small hearts border = 1 Butterfly.

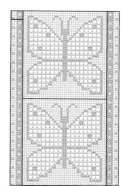

MIX & MATCH Add vertical bands of Spotted stripe allover pattern (page 64). 10 repeats of Spotted stripe = 1 Butterfly.

STITCH KEY ☐ Space ■ Block ⊠ Lacet and bar

SEE ALSO
Lacets, bars, and diamond
lacets, page 22
Using the designs, page 26
Planning a design, page 28

Alphabet and numbers

Personalize your gifts for friends and family by adding, names, initials, dates, or special messages. Use the charted letters and numbers to draw your own chart for any name or message you want, as shown below. You will need graph paper and a pencil.

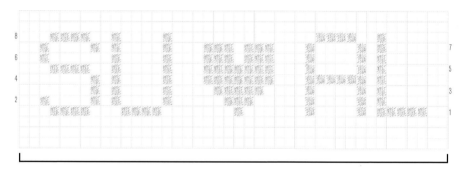

38 mesh squares

Copy the letters and/or numbers you want onto the graph paper, leaving one empty square between letters. If you want more than one word or name, leave two or three squares between them. You can also include suitable motifs, such as this Small heart from the border on page 77. Count the total number of mesh squares required for the width, and number the rows as shown. Place the design wherever you want on your project.

MIX & MATCH
These initials and small heart motif could be used for a project such as a pillow, and perhaps given as a wedding gift.

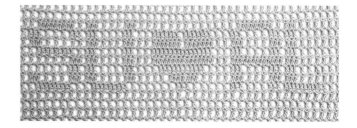

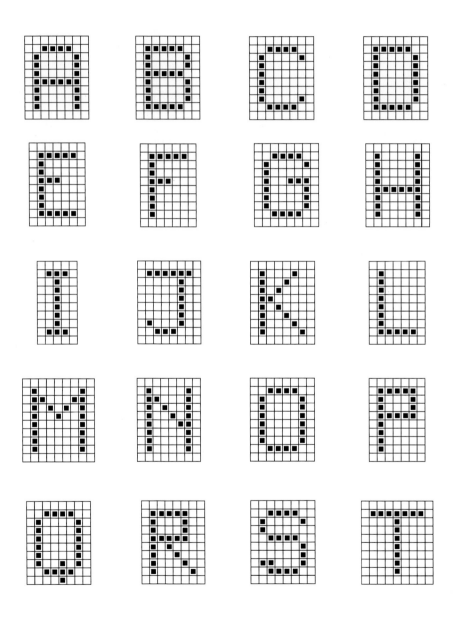

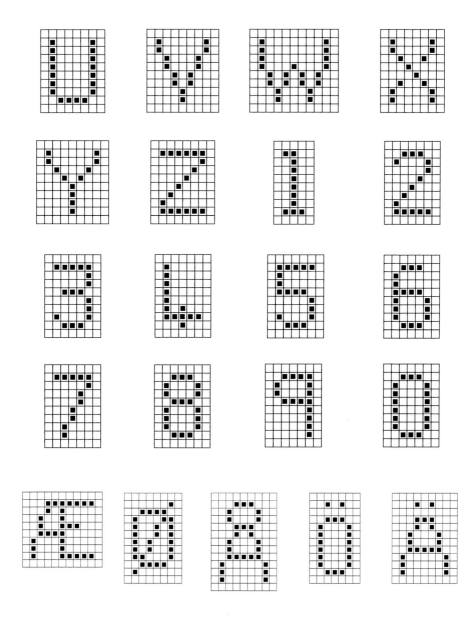

Crochet aftercare

Once a project is completed, it's important always to follow the yarn manufacturer's laundering instructions and to store crocheted pieces carefully and appropriately.

Looking after crochet

Follow the laundering and pressing instructions on the ball band for the particular yarn you have used. If the yarn is machine-washable, put the item into a zip-up mesh laundry bag to prevent stretching and snagging during the wash cycle. If you don't have a mesh bag, you can use a clean white pillowcase instead; simply secure the open end with an elastic hair band or work a row of running stitches across the opening to close the pillowcase. If you have household items such as tablecloths or tray cloths trimmed with crochet, treat spills and stains as soon as they occur and repair any damage to the crochet fabric before laundering the item.

For crochet pieces made from yarns which are not machine-washable, wash carefully by hand in hand-hot water with a mild, detergent-free cleaning agent. Most specialist wool or fabric shampoos are ideal, but check that the one you choose does not contain optical brighteners that will cause yarn colors to fade. Rinse the piece thoroughly in several changes of water the same temperature as the washing water to avoid felting. Carefully squeeze as much surplus water out as you can, without wringing, then roll the damp item in a towel and press to remove more moisture. Gently ease the item into shape and dry flat out of direct sunlight. Follow the instructions on the ball band for pressing once the item is dry.

Fiber content of yarn

Washing and pressing instructions

Weight and length of yarn ball

Shade and dye lot numbers

HAND WASHING	MACHINE WASHING	BLEACHING	PRESSING	DRY CLEANING
⊠ DO NOT WASH BY HAND OR MACHINE	86°F 〈30〉 MACHINE WASHABLE IN WARM WATER AT STATED TEMPERATURE	⊠ BLEACHING NOT PERMITTED	⊠ DO NOT PRESS	⊗ DO NOT DRY CLEAN
			◁ PRESS WITH A COOL IRON	Ⓐ May be dry cleaned with all solutions
⊡ HAND WASHABLE IN WARM WATER AT STATED TEMPERATURE	86°F 〈30〉 MACHINE WASHABLE IN WARM WATER AT STATED TEMPERATURE, COOL RINSE AND SHORT SPIN	△CL BLEACHING PERMITTED (WITH CHLORINE)	◁ PRESS WITH A WARM IRON	Ⓟ May be dry cleaned with perchlorethylene or fluorocarbon or petroleum-based solvents
				Ⓕ May be dry cleaned with fluorocarbon or petroleum-based solvents only
	104°F 〈40〉 MACHINE WASHABLE IN WARM WATER AT STATED TEMPERATURE, SHORT SPIN		◁ PRESS WITH A HOT IRON	

LAUNDERING SYMBOLS
Always check the yarn ball band for washing and pressing instructions. Standard laundering symbols as used on ball bands can be seen above.

Storing crochet

The main enemies of crochet fabrics—apart from dust and dirt—are direct sunlight, which can cause yarn colors to fade and fibers to weaken; excess heat which makes yarn dry and brittle; damp, which rots fibers and moths which can seriously damage woolen yarns. Avoid storing yarns or finished crochet items for any length of time in polythene bags as the polythene attracts dirt and dust, which will transfer readily to your work.

Polythene also prevents yarns containing natural fibers such as cotton and linen from breathing, which can result in mildew attacks and eventually weaken or rot the fibers. Instead, store small items wrapped in white, acid-free tissue paper or an old cotton pillowcase. For large heavy items such as winter-weight jackets and sweaters, which might drop and stretch out of shape if stored on clothes hangers, fold them loosely between layers of white tissue paper, making sure that each fold is padded with tissue. Store all the items in a drawer, cupboard or other dark, dry, and moth-free place and check them regularly, refolding larger items. It's also a good idea to make small fabric bags filled with dried lavender flowers to tuck into the drawer or cupboard with your crochet as the smell deters moths.

Working the charts

Fold out this flap for an at-a-glance reminder on how to work any chart in the book.

Working the charts

The chart below provides a quick reference on exactly how to work filet crochet on small, medium, and large meshes.

SYMBOL		SMALL MESH	MEDIUM MESH	LARGE MESH
(no symbol)	foundation chain (page 11)	2 ch per chart square	3 ch per chart square	3 ch per chart square
(no symbol)	turning chain (page 14)	3 ch	3 ch	4ch
☐	space (page 17)	1 ch, 1 dc	2 ch, 1 dc	2 ch, 1 tr
■	block (page 17)	2 dc	3 dc	3 tr
∨	lacet (pages 22–23)	2 ch, 1 sc, 2 ch, 1 dc	3 ch, 1 sc, 3 ch, 1 dc	4 ch, 1 sc, 4 ch, 1 tr
—	bar (pages 22–23)	3 ch, 1 dc	5 ch, 1 dc	5 ch, 1 tr
∧	reverse lacet (pages 22–23)	1 ch, 2 dc tog, 1 ch, 1 dc	2 ch, 2 tr tog, 2 ch, 1 dc	2 ch, 2 dtr tog, 2 ch, 1 tr

Abbreviations

These are the abbreviations used in this book. There is no worldwide standard, so, in other publications you may find different abbreviations.

ABBREVIATIONS USED IN THIS BOOK	
ch	chain
ch sp	chain space
dc	double crochet
dtr	double treble
sc	single crochet
ss	slipstitch
st(s)	stitch(es)
tr	treble
yrh	yarn round hook

American/English terminology

The patterns in this book use American terminology. Patterns published using English terminology can be very confusing because some English terms differ from the American system, as shown below:

AMERICAN	ENGLISH
Single crochet (sc)	Double crochet (dc)
Half double crochet (hdc)	Half treble crochet (htr)
Double crochet (dc)	Treble crochet (tr)
Treble crochet (tr)	Double treble crochet (dtr)
Double treble crochet (dtr)	Triple treble crochet (ttr)

Index